Hide

Hide

Angela France

ISBN: 978-0-9573847-1-2

Scan QR code for further title information

Copyright © Angela France, 2013

Cover photograph © Eleanor Bennett
www.eleanorleonnebennett.zenfolio.com

Author photograph © Derek Adams
www.derekadamsphotography.com

First published March 2013 by:

Nine Arches Press
Great Central Studios
92 Lower Hillmorton Rd
Rugby, Warwickshire
CV21 3TF

www.ninearchespress.com

Printed in Britain by:

imprintdigital.net
Seychelles Farm,
Upton Pyne,
Exeter
EX5 5HY
www.imprintdigital.net

Hide

Angela France

Nine
Arches
Press

Angela France has had poems published in many of the leading journals, both in the UK and abroad, and has been anthologised a number of times. She has an MA in 'Creative and Critical Writing' from the University of Gloucestershire and is studying for a PhD. Her previous publications include *Occupation* (Ragged Raven Press) and *Lessons in Mallemaroking* (Nine Arches Press). Angela France is also features editor of *Iota* and runs a monthly poetry cafe, 'Buzzwords'; *Hide* is her third full collection of poetry.

CONTENTS

PROSPECT

Peer into hedgerows,
part thickets and look
in their dark centres,
trail through pine woods,
kick through leaves under beech trees.
  Clear the ditches,
drag the pond, examine each tangle
of weed and scrap of metal,
use a pole to prod deep
until you know there's nothing there.
  Check the outhouses;
move the old bikes, the mower,
the paint cans and scraps of wood.
Rake through the dusty nuggets
of coal in the corner, pull cobwebs
away from the shelves, ignore
gritty smears on your hands.
  Go home. Search the cellar,
the attic, pull out boxes from under beds,
chests from closets. Look inside.
Learn to wait.

URSA

At first just a blur of outline, then sprouting
to shaggy brown. The knarl of exposed roots soften,
flatten to wide feet, pushing against the earth

to straighten the bowed back.
                              A stub of fallen branch
lengthens to a broad muzzle and a lightning-struck
split in the bole forms front legs with strong,
round paws. She shakes free

                of the last branches and drops
to stand on all fours, yawns a long-toothed roar
and stretches sinew and bone awake.

She steps away from the litter of twigs and leaves,
her must gathering strength to rise;
pine and oestrus, sweet and pungent.

She ambles down the slope, deliberate, unhurried,
muscles sliding under her rough hide,
paws heavy on the ground, the curve of claw
tearing through turf.

She turns her head to look over the arc
of her shoulder, knows I'm watching.

I don't have cunning enough
to follow her, not this time,
                not in this place.

Hoard

Berries blacken and gloss in the late sun,
tempting past any memory of thorns
or scratched shins and my urge to pick them
is sharp as hunger; I need to collect
the mushrooms that glimmer like small moons
in half-light, newspaper-wrap apples
to layer in a tea chest, bottle, blanch
and freeze until it no longer matters
how long, or cold, the winter to come.

GETTING HERE FROM THERE

I name where I tread
grass, rock, mud
to fix the ground beneath me.

A door ajar.
Inside, a smell of emptiness,
a taste of waiting; logs stacked
by the grate, blankets folded on a bed.

On the mantelpiece, a cracked mirror
and a bottle holding a curl of dark hair.
A book lies on the table, my name
on the cover, its pages blank.
The wall opposite the window
has nails knocked into a beam
to hold a large map
                of my skin.

I stay the day, studying the map.
          And I stay the days after,
learning the setting of each mole
and freckle, rebuilding
an inch at a time.

When the hair in the bottle is streaked
with grey, I wash and fold blankets,
sweep the grate, chop logs to stack.
I take down the map, roll it
to fit my backpack, pocket the bottle,
leave the door ajar.

SIGHTLINES

I who is not-I bolts like a day-caught fox
from the path; a fire-streak across the field
taking my breath to ground.

It settles here, between my eye
and a bank of dead nettles where brambled
lines spin a loose weave of risk.

I write of cloud leaving the hill,
how it straggles in tree-tops,
tattered fleece on a fence.
I slip into skins and stretch
inside disguises or practise voices
                with my tongue folded.

I should be facing back through stories
of shortening days and wind-chime bones,
leaving the rain to wash a year's dust
from the leaves or turning over stones
in a bowl, finding unexpected glints.

            The exit wound appears after
            a moment of change
                    like a paper-cut
                    until blood seeps along the line,
                    or a bruise which blooms
                    with no memory of pain.

I who is not-I slips into Jackdaw skin,
shrugs grey shoulders, sleeks black hood,
cocks a pale eye.
                        This I rattles feathers,
steals scraps of song, trills ringtones
and a builder's whistle, free-falls from a tree-top,
tumbles to stir a cloud, flicks a wing-tip.
                        This I stores pretty things,
pecks a split or turn, makes patterns
on beech bark to twist in the wind.

Jackdaws chuckle into high branches
for the night, leave I who is not-I
to scratch jagged lines
                        on the ground.

            From my shoulder, a susurration
            in Doppler effect, directing focus
            to a vein on a leaf, a hilltop tree,
            a half-heard conversation:
            Just this, just this.

I who is not-I knows what stirs at 3 am,
waits outside to watch bats
wink flickers of absence from air.
Turns away from night-scented blooms,
follows lanes clouded by blind walls
to shadowed corners where fears
take icy forms and town foxes skulk
behind bins.

This I knows back ways
into the churchyard, hears tilting stones
breathe worn names and picks through grass
for lost bones. This I knows thistles grow
on newly dug ground.

All the 'I's line up, stripe my view
in lines of darkness and light,
striate the landscape.
Hard rain on a window,
split sunbeams on a floor,
cracks on a mirror,
multiple and refracting.

ANAGNORISIS

Connective tissue creaks between ribs
and marrow shudders in long bones,
shy of the narrowing search. It's not there,

among the rigid and gristle of skeletal frames
nor under locked skull-seams; not nestled
in a palm, though my fingers curl into shelter.

My belly's complacent spread has room
to offer soft harbour and the careless attitude
of years; my spine feels shifty, stiff with suspicion.

My only surety is carbon and water, ashes;
language as sensation,
                                    no words.

Canzone: Cunning

My marrow is veined with cunning;
history is written in our bones.
Not sneaky, like a fox, sort of cunning
nor a neat design sort of cunning;
not an adjective, but a title given
or grown into. A different cunning
which forms in the gut; a cunning
earning a capital over hard-worn time.
A woman, or man, doesn't count time
until someone calls *Hey, Cunning!*
It's not me they call but an old woman
who runs in my veins, a cunning woman.

You always knew what you were, old woman.
I grew knowing the wink of your cunning,
the cackle and knock of a comfortable woman
who had aged past appearances. Oh, woman,
your grin seeded such an itch in my bones
to plant my feet on dark earth, to be a woman
who lives in her own skin, a woman
who pricks importance with profanity. It's given
a sense of the lightness that held you, given
me the weight of what it means to be woman,
to skate before the pressure-wave of passing time,
to harvest and hoard the gathering marks of time.

When everything was beginning, time
was a kaleidoscope. Becoming a woman
seemed just out of reach, fragments of time
spun away by wishing. Naïve of the tricks time
plays, it took years to match it in cunning;
stretching when I wanted it to shrink, time
raced on when I wanted to hold it still. Time
teases with knowledge growing as bones
weaken; by the time I felt in my bones
who and where I needed to be, time
had already taken more of the years given
than there were years left still to be given.

It's too easy to forget what we're given
by old women over the cradle, betting against time.
But I recall the nudge, wink, and grin I was given
when you won at cards or your steady look, given
to me when you saw shade over a man, or woman,
and knew they'd come to the end of the time given.
You never told what you'd given,
left in trust to mature into cunning.
Before I could name it, I knew your cunning
had come to me; knew something had been given,
passed down. I knew it in the grinding of my bones
but had no word for it until it had worn my bones

to creaking. There's little spring left in my bones,
lines map my skin to trace all I've given
and I feel my flesh hang heavy on my bones.
In the mirror, I see you in the shape of my bones,
in the length of my nose, in the weight time
leaves on me. I hear the rattle of your bones
and feel you chuckle when I see you in my bones;
when I was young, you were always old, woman,
but I'm where you were and don't feel an old woman.
Years slip through my fingers, gravity drags at bones;
I don't fear getting old if it comes with your cunning;
your shape, your heft, your cunning.

Not an adjective, not sneaky-like-a-fox cunning;
but the cunning in the sight of a comfortable woman
who has accepted her indenture to time,
who has lifted the lid on what was long given,
who knows what quickens in the marrow of our bones.

Doppelgänger

She is anywhere before me
tying thread on significant twigs
                    or following behind
leaving trails of white pebbles
                    like landing lights
or paper lanterns marking a garden path

I see her slant   a flicker at the edge of vision
when I'm alone   a hint of shadow in company

She scratches at my window when I'm working
                grins out from behind the eyes
of the woman I pass on the hill who holds a gate
and smiles me through
                grey hair wiry below her hat
                    a collie at her heel
and in the sharp glance of a crow
                rag-tagging down from a tree

I hear her mutter as she hoards memory
    gathers snatches of conversation   watches
                            the street

Family Visits

Quiet now. It's their turn to visit;
the old aunts and uncles, the great
and grand parents. They visit as we did
—rarely and politely, quiet as we were
in their musty houses where
we were fascinated into silence
by great age, a pendulous lip
or skin like crumpled tissue.

They come singly, slipping in
unnoticed, content to perch on a bed
or lean on a mantelpiece
until they're seen. They don't speak,
don't change position, only nod
or gesture at a picture, a fireplace,
or a vase of flowers, seeding.

HIDE

The wallpaper peeled easily;
long strips fell away, weighted with dust
and lime. Near the top of the stairs
a half-door appeared, its latch removed,
its shape disguised between panels
of lath and plaster. It opened
to an angled space, loose boards
for a floor, sacking tacked to roof beams.

> I have always craved secret places:
> rooms within walls, smugglers' tunnels,
> the bookcase that glides sideways
> for a knowing touch. I tap on trees
> hoping for hollows and slip behind
> garden shrubs, seeking a path
> to snake across boundaries.

I crawl into that place
under the eaves, lie on the boards
to feel their edges rib my back;
stretch a measure of length
then bend up my knees,
span my arms, palm to brick,
fingertip to rafter.

> I fray hessian away from a nail,
> chip a corner, spy a crack or slipped tile
> to claim a slice of sky.
> I wait out seasons for a day
> when clouds bloom into stories
> or scud before the wind; watch
> swifts skirl overhead, oblivious
> to my hungry eye.

Some of These Things are True

I learned about waiting, the sour tang of it
I had long conversations with my bicycle
I lived in a cave, learned the rhythms of bats
I stopped whispering, tongued the roundness of breath
I discovered a mad child and held the door open
I spoke a long truth and lived with it

I discovered an ocean with too many waves and no shore
I built a shelter in the valley, roofed it with paper
I wore khaki and army boots, but couldn't keep in step
I learned to walk on stilts, saw a different horizon
I found a new land with no borders, no checkpoints
I told a lie and gagged at the lingering taste

I learned about weight and what I could carry
I swam a sea and found a lake within it
I counted rats running from a dog in the stable
I cut through strands and tangles, took longer strides
I lived on a cliff-edge, looked down every morning
I made a people, named each one a colour

I sipped at displacement, turned it over on my tongue
I watched a fox stalk a goose, counted leaves on clover
I found a hidden door, felt a songbird fly from my hand.

The Visit

Brown is the colour of waiting; a wainscot in a dingy room,
straight-backed chairs against the wall, tweed coats

on old women whose felt hats nod in approval and tilt
towards each other. They lean together to whisper

lineage, connections; which daughter, whose son, what cousin
is parent to the child who holds her grandmother's hand

as she's led through to the inner room. Beyond the door,
an old man leans from a narrow bed and the colours of dying

are yellow and white. A sheet winds round him, rumples
to leave a scrawny leg exposed, jaundiced against the linen

and his stained beard quivers as he mumbles over the bowl
held by a shadowy woman who counts his golden breaths.

LIVING WITH THE SOOTERKIN

Every home has them, nesting in dark corners
or playing in the rafters; dusty grey faces
peeping from under beds and round chair legs.

Sooterkin are sly, secretive about their long lives,
their complicated families. No-one knows
why they migrate at random times of year

or why they breed in some houses, congregate
in others. I'm on to them; I glimpse their sharp faces
at dusk as they slip along the skirting, see glints

from black eyes on my back seat when I drive
at night. Sooterkin are bold in the dark;
anxiety excites them; they chitter in packs,

sliding over and under each other, claws tapping
a tarantella on the floor. They grow strong on insomnia;
slither over the bed-head, under the covers, tangle

my hair with their long toes, tease bare skin
with soft whiskers. They communicate in scuffles
and squeaks at the edge of hearing; I am learning

their language, studying scratches on the floor
and recording nocturnal creaks. I can read
their discomfort growing; they don't like to be known.
I think they'll leave.

Spy

The top class's cloakroom
was best, where the coats were long
enough to skim the bench.
I squatted behind them,
breathing a fug
of duffel and gabardine,
listening for codes.

I practised whispering silently
into my walkie-talkie.
In the corridors,
learned to walk quietly,
finger-tipped the wall,
reported the ebb and flow
of allegiances.

I moved among them
to learn playground games
and language, overheard
some boys
she's mad, she is,
talks to herself all day!

I radioed that my cover
was secure;
they think I'm mad;
didn't wait for an answer.

Forgotten Trails

Favourite scarves on park benches,
umbrellas in cabs, books loaned
to too-casual acquaintances or left
on trains. Coats left in restaurants,
sunglasses on a beach, hairbrushes
in hotel bathrooms.

They trail behind me, ghostly
outlines in a fading contrail,
skittering on sharp turns,
stretching thin when I travel fast.

I could follow the trail back to rented rooms
where forgetting leached to grey
or steamy kitchens of shouted numbers.
I could track it to school buildings
where the smells of chalk and fear blend
and cloy in the throat, or to small churches
– dark and bible-dusty.

Along the trail, figures stand, still.
Some are complete, a few are vague shapes,
others have faces blurred by the mist.
Voices weave between them; detached,
rising and falling, occasional words
suddenly clear; bubbles rising in a swamp;
sparks from logs shifting on a fire.

SCAPEGOAT

turns away from pastures
pulls at bitter scrub & yellowed grass
limps over sharp-edged stones
& shifting shale   He backs from
clean waters   mumbles cracked lips
at stagnant pools where sulphured
bubbles rise & release miasmic gas
Scapegoat trails his shaggy coat
through swamps & noxious bogs
braces his knees against the weight
of drying mud & caked slime
turns away from sheltered caves
& soft leaf beds   lies on a jut of rock
above the canyon where icy wind
buffets & blows grit into his eyes
bows his head

HOMECOMING

Some of our dead return, they must.
An old woman won't leave her cunning;
she clings to the hearth, the smoulder
of soot on the fireback as it catches
and shifts in ragged lines.
                          She comes to creak
the door of the kitchen corner cupboard,
sustained on the breath of cold stone,
the slab where marks hold a memory
of skinned conies, the high shelf for jars.
She'll bring the cards to the top of the deck,
the flinch of superstitions, the sigh in the night.

The old man stays in the garden;
rustles the apple tree for pruning and blows
leaves around a fork left outside. He measures
digging to a spit and a half, calls for potatoes to plant
at new moon and counts seeds in threes
to give Old Nick and the birds their dues.
At night he's a crackle of paper he couldn't read,
the tap of a pipe, the grumble of poor coal on the fire.

Not madeleines,

but damp bricks in small spaces,
light rain on rusty tin, coal-dust
in the kitchen, good earth
on potatoes in the sink.

The front door opens
— a pig's head grins from the table,
blind to the budgie cage and china
horses on the sideboard.
Brasses hang on the chimney-breast,
details rubbed to soft focus.
A snaffle bit dangles in the alcove
by the 1914 tobacco tin,
a biscuit tin of buttons, a kilner jar
of bolts, buckles and old keys.
Wooden-armed chairs, straight backs
pressed to the wall, leave room
to sidle around the table to the fire
with a bucket of coal.

There's no lounging;
only space to sit up straight, upright
as the ladder-steep stairs which climb
between two rooms; as the sun-denying
brick wall around the yard; as the old man's
suspicion of book-learning.

Dogma

The things he held sacred:
      a drilled rank of bean-sticks
      potato mounds in die-straight lines
      clean tools stacked in the lean-to
      shed on the allotment.
The doorstep of the tiny house
      shined cardinal red
      the fire well banked at night
      gleaming windows and door-brass
      children inspected before school
      neat, respectable.
The King's Arms on the corner
      the racing pages in the newspaper
      a pint of dark ale in his tankard
      the company of other men
      who believe a man's worthy of his hire
      and what he earns is his to spend.

WHAT IS HIDDEN

So many small lives, pushing through
soil below our feet; cogs within
clocks; wintering bees; the black skin
of polar bears; the missing screw;
the way I still feel about you.
How swifts live a whole life in flight;
the words in a book when the light
is out; squirrels' hoards; the odd sock;
the sculpture in a rough wood block;
what terrors wake me through the night.

Private View

    Faint shapes flicker behind the glass;
a baby in a coach-built pram peeps through spots
in the silvering, a solemn child with cropped hair
fades behind a mist of dust. Jagged cracks disrupt
rows of desks and hard faces; a birthday party
passes an endless parcel; a teenager staggers
from a club, swaying in and out of focus
and a bridal veil webs
                    a shattered surface.

All the mirrors are in a room with no windows
hidden in the centre of the house, the door disguised
with paint and shelves. They hang on every wall,
lean in stacks at the skirting and cluster on tables,
no two the same. Plain wooden frames, ornate squares
with gilded, dusty curls, silver ovals, full length
and hand-sized.

Some gleam in soft focus, polished with each glance;
a beribboned bunch of flowers on a doorstep,
a golden-haired child on a lap, rows of smiling faces,
clapping hands. In every corner mirrors reflect
each other, refract distorted glimpses to repeat
and reprise but some mirrors are empty,
                            unmarked.

SAM BROWNE

Brasso-silky fingertips, a metal tang in the throat;
tiny circles on the buckle and tongue-tip between my teeth

to guard against marks on the leather. He smiles
at my effort, shows me how he buffs to perfection

and I watch him thread the strap under an epaulette,
fasten the buckles so it sits high on his waist,

his jacket smooth beneath it and close on his wide chest.
I breathe *my dad* as he straightens his cap over his eyes.

He takes as much care with a security guard uniform;
irons a shirt, makes knife-edge creases on trouser legs

with wet cloth under a sizzling iron, polishes each button
to mirror the sun. He reaches for the clothes brush

from a hook by the door, kept for rebel dog hairs,
turns and laughs loud to see his Sam Browne

a perfect fit on my teenage hips. I scowl, flounce
through the door, the belt snug and heavy on my pelvis.

I don't remember when I saw it last,
tarnished and cracked for lack of army discipline;

tan leather and the smell of metal polish bring it to mind
with broad shoulders, strong hands, a sad falling in.

Lǎo tóng

For C.

I loosen the earth with a fork,
bend to pull weeds, grub my fingers down

to find roots but I'm impatient, slapdash,
don't pick out all the white threads

that hold the promise of next year's weeds.
I think of you, telling me you liked kneeling

by your long border, seeking out every blade
of grass, every weed and fine root.

In your studio, brushes bloom from a pot,
graded from broad strokes to barely visible

sable, just enough for you to paint a hair
on a poppy stem or a cell in a moth's eye.

For all we shared, all the ways we were alike,
it is the opposites in you I miss the most

and I can't help wishing you more careless
with roots, that you'd left behind a thread

to bring you back next year.

*Lǎo tóng is an archaic Chinese word for form of eternal friendship
between "heart sisters" — two women who were closer than husband
and wife.*

Counting the Cunning Ways

Corpse-hounds, he calls them or *lych-birds*,
turns away from their churring call. He curses
a white moth in the house, slaps at its blunder
against a dusty bulb. He'll take a long way round
to avoid meeting a hearse head-on, shudder
to see a child point at the plumed horses.
He won't take the ashes out after sundown,
always comes and goes by the same door,
shouts at ravens to chase them from the roof.
He won't wear anything new to a funeral
and covers his head by an open grave.
The bird in the house, the left eye's twitch,
hawthorn indoors, a mirror cracked
—so many ways to foretell death and disaster;
it came for him while he wasn't looking.

SLOW WAYS

Early this morning, a slow-worm,
a bronze coil shining through the dense
ivy tangled beneath a fence.
At my slightest touch it moved, firm
and cool, more like a wheel's turn
than a slither or slide. I drew
the leaves aside, watched it slip through
snarls of vine as if a clear trail
formed where it chose to go, its tail
a last flick as it passed from view.

Thinking back, it's years since I've seen
those smooth coils, that muscular form,
though I often walk where gnats swarm
while high umbels nod and trees lean
over the cut, a stencilled screen
for the sky. An age since I'd play
with such creatures, make bouquets
of cow-parsley and willowherb
with no sense of time to disturb
the slow worm of long green days.

PETRICHOR

The door stands open to stillness and heat.
Only gnats move, ghosting under trees
and dipping over the pond. Birds murmur
in the hedge, flutter and settle; leaves droop
under the weight of air   and so do I.

Rain spots the path, penny-sized, darkening.
A lock falls away from a crowbar,
a crack splits a geode's dull crust,
a caul tears from a new calf. It breaks.
The earth breathes   and so do I.

Spatial Awareness

In the space before sleep you learn
I has no voice.
                    You reach for a tongue,
find it split into ribbons, slippery
tangles with no ends;
                    thoughts dissolve
into the thump and rush of arteries,
settle on to the heaviness of bone.
Only the body doesn't lie.

To preserve this space
            you must feel, but not notice
how mahogany bedposts soften and curve
as the bed's corners curl up and in,
            a cradle
                    or a boat
or a falling leaf; don't acknowledge
the way it rocks, don't recognise
the voices that sometimes call
your name.
            To stay here, in this space,
practice the art of slovenly attention.

THE EVOLUTION OF INSOMNIA

Men don't tend the fire;
they follow their spear-points
to the hunt's rank heat and fury,
limp back to fall into sleep
filled with fight and fear.
They don't make old bones.

Younger women are busy
with breast-suck or belly-weight;
their gaze on the seeking and keeping
of a mate. They watch the fire
between other demands, attention
like sparks from green wood.

Past child-bearing, past mate-catching,
older women give their nights
to the fire, stare into the flame
and serve its sullen greed. They learn
to doze and wake through the dark hours,
leave behind the feel of long sleep.

Awake in fidgety heat at 3 am,
I know it started with fire, the mystery
and need of it, its fickle demands;
I know it's my place to foster the blaze
and watch the coming dark.

LATE BUS

The shiver-chill and diesel stink of the late bus;
the taste of a dull day in my mouth

and the lights tinting road-grime on the windows
to yellow. Outside, stores close and shutters rattle.

From the lit bus, everything looks darker
and where it stops, damp paving seems to shudder.

Seats empty as it nears the end of the route
and streets quieten so that it's forty years back,

trailing home after a detention,
not wanting to arrive.

SCHOOL FOR IDENTITY THIEVES

Expression is forbidden.
First years struggle to flatten smiles,
freeze brows; admire the seniors
whose faces have perfected vacancy.

History lessons list great imposters;
Princess Caraboo, Sidney Poitier's son,
and the man who sold the Eiffel Tower.
Students research family trees,
copy birth certificates, tour graveyards.
Their own family histories
are discouraged, visits forbidden.

Invisibility must be achieved for success;
classes in stillness, shrinking and fading
into backgrounds begin each day.
New students watch a graduation ceremony
as a teacher talks to a room of shadows.
Some have a natural talent
for not being noticed.

Now, Under the Trees

I could practice blindness as the canopy drips in my eyes
and not-knowing as tree becomes all I touch; could rise
with the sap through branch to twig, fragment and divide,

split around whorls in the heart-wood, leave solidity behind
to weigh the roots down with logic, find lightness in travelling
to fine ends where leaves burst from buds and only the smallest

birds can perch to feed. I could become tree and twig,
songbird and owl, and learn to know nothing of what feet feel
from the ground, if I lay down in the rain, now, under the trees.

STOLEN

Someone took my name today.
I heard her speak it at the ticket window
while I stood in line. I saw her on the train,
facing me through glass, across the buffers,
watching me   watching her.

She's getting off at the same station,
steps down with her right foot
          as I lead with my left;
follows me up the steps
but a shimmy through the cab rank
and a risky dash across traffic
      loses her on the street.

All through town I jitter
at reflections, listen hard to words
surfacing in fragments through engine-revs
or music leaking from noisy shops.
A dozen times I glimpse a partial profile,
a way of walking, and side-step into doorways
       or turn down alleys.

I try the taste of my name
in my mouth as a child knows a thing
by naming it.
     The doorbell shocks
my breath short; the handle rattles.
       I turn the key.

CUNNING

The potatoes planted on a new moon. New shoes
never on the table. The colour green kept from the house.

A coat never laid on a bed. White lilac held separate
from mauve. The luck that shouldn't be named.

The handshake away from the table. The china horses
turned from the door. The broom never leant on a bed.

Fingernail clippings always thrown on the fire. Breath held
at the cemetery gate. The doors unlocked for a death.

The trick on the doorstep. Pepper under a pillow.
The cards that always turn up in time.

An unseen gesture. The string on the banister.
Ashes in the graveyard. The wink at church carvings.

    The wind you can't stop from blowing,
    how you say it always sobs your name.

THUMB-PRICKS & EYE-DAZZLES

Peeling boiled eggs; the prick of eggshell
on my thumb warns of warts, of witches
sailing away on half-shells, of the dangers
in egg-water, of *by the pricking of my thumbs*.
It's like the stretch of my hand around
a too-big potato and the feel of the waxed
twine on the peeler handle; the sink
I lean on becomes deep and square,
cracks spidering from the drain, the scent
of damp earth rising from the peelings.
Or it's like the sudden dazzle of autumn
sun which sends me back in to a dream
I had once, of a songbird trapped
in my house, the frantic soft flutter
of it in my hands; of opening a door
to release it and being blinded by light
so that all I could see was my hand
fading into white and the pomegranate
squint of my eyelids. As the small weight
left my hand, I couldn't see
whether it flew or fell.

Other tongues

When I say I'm alone, I'm lying.
My mother tongue sleeps under my skin,
bred in the bone, colouring my blood.
I speak from an echo chamber
where the walls pulse with whispers,
familiar cadences rising and falling
at my back. I speak from a limestone floor,
as familiar to my feet as are the bones
of the hill creaking between the roots
of great beeches. I speak with multitudes
in my throat, their round vowels
vibrating in my stomach, their pitch
and tone stiffening my spine.

WINDOW SEAT

The local train rattles
along a wide bend;
half-term children cluster
to windows on the left
where a dull sea grumbles.

Electric ribbon flutters
on drunken spikes,
ponies dot the ground;
piebald, skewbald, shaggy duns,
stand with their tails to the wind
or pull at scrub.

Five railway carriages;
liveries of faded green and cream,
each standing on rails
cut to carriage length.
I can see through the windows
most of the seats removed;
a cooker, a bed, a man busy
with wood and tools,
a woman sitting at a table,
watching us pass,
life framed in a train window
as if always travelling.

But would you go back?

                    Would you
button up your coat and go back
to the house with the blue door
to sit at the drop-leaf table
where you must temper
the Sunday tinned fruit treat
with bread and margarine.
Would you lie in a narrow bed
and listen to coals being raked
downstairs, knowing you're late,
you'll miss the early bus that would
get you there in time to claim a space
in the corner of the schoolyard
where girls lean on the coal bunkers
and watch the gates for targets.
Would you return to the mirrors
in the town hall cloakroom, look
sideways at what the others do
with make-up while you fiddle
with your hair and all the time
know that it's never enough;
                    not ever.

NANNA'S LUCK

The rabbit's foot in her pocket
was capped in silver, grey fur
sleek from fingering; the four-leafed clover
in her purse flattened paper-thin.
She refused to call it luck or cunning,
only winked at her cronies
when they called her a jammy beggar.

I'd sit with her at the curved counter
in the holiday camp, sliding plastic shutters
as she pointed to numbers when they came up,
waiting for her to shout *House!*
Mum sat there too, listening to the caller
legs eleven, two little ducks, key of the door,
and grumbling that the numbers didn't come
for her. Nanna told her to concentrate;
you ent thinkin' right!

There was a day when I spent hours on my knees,
counting leaves on clover, looking for the one
which would lend strength, bolster radiation,
shrink tumours. I found one; perfectly shaped,
each leaf the same size and set at ninety degrees
to its neighbour. She tucked it in her purse
and grinned. It didn't work; we weren't
thinking right.

Roots

I have earth under my nails, grimed into knuckles
and lining my palms as a benediction. My back aches
with the memory of digging, resists the instinct to stand tall.

Raw holes colander the garden, gape ragged-lipped at the house,
boxes stacked at windows, charity shop bags muffling the door.

I carry uprooted flowers to your house; bend with the weight
of the message you didn't read in the books, the discs
or the old photographs. I don't know if you can understand
the generation in absence.

ORPHAN ASHES

These youngsters, shallow of root
and thin of bark, are far from
the Tree of the World; they'll split
no bole to cradle a rickety child nor drop
their keys to heal a gout. They grow
away from fevers, infections, dropsy
or stitch; they'll lend no leaves
to the snake-bit, protect no hearts.
They've shared no honey to seal
a family, have no place to call home.
All image, all appearance, they can only
spread harm where they roam.

Decent

All are welcome at the altar
of the small god of decent people.
Cloakrooms in the entrance hall
are provided for coats and shoes
which are not plain and sensible.

Customary segregation
offers entry through appropriate
vestibules; the women's has water,
coal-tar soap and rough towels
to ensure clean, shining faces at the rail.
The men's has a barber-attendant
to offer shaves, hair-length check
and smoothing of unsuitable styles.

Our temples contain no distractions;
magnolia walls and frosted windows
discourage cloud watching, wondering,
                    or wool-gathering.

The small god of decent people
is not against recreation;
our summer picnic in the country
is popular for wholesome games,
fishpaste sandwiches and Madeira cake.
Well-behaved children may get a portion
of ice cream, served with bread and margarine,
to reinforce their parents'
          training in decent living
                    without fanciful ostentation.

REASONABLE

The Man on the Clapham Omnibus, to a lawyer, is synonymous with the pinnacle of reason in humanity: an ordinary London transit rider as representative of all rational thought and action. — Gray's Law Dictionary

The man on the Clapham omnibus is tired
    of being reasonable. He is bored
with his average intelligence and sees little use
    for being moderately educated.

 From the window he can see tidy houses,
    rows of cars parked at the kerb.
He wants to jump from the bus while it's moving,
    run along the roofs and bonnets,

tap-dance to feel the satisfying dint and ping
    while he yodels a rebellion. He wants
to leap over hedges and walls, bang on every door,
    laugh from the far side of the road.

Tomorrow, he will wear an eye-patch and fix
    a stuffed rat to his shoulder.
He'll stand on the bus to declaim Shakespeare
    on his way to the library

to become an expert on *New Guinea Tapeworms*
    or *Fungi on Stamps*. He'll share
his knowledge in the café for several hours
    before he goes home to rest

on his doorstep with a beer bottle in his hand
    and Handel's *Messiah* at full volume.
He'll shout occasional phrases from *Zadok the Priest*;
    no-one will interrupt him.

Scapula:

I like the shape
of the word in my mouth. The sharp angle
of its beginning, its fulsome end.
I like the planes of them,
the sigh of their support as I relax against a wall,
the flat surface they offer to the sun.
I like the way they lie,
mirrored either side of my spine,
how they slide under my skin as I move,
how they quietly hold the potential of wings.

WILLOW

won't die.
Felled by lightning-strike or chainsaw,
split by weight or wind, bridged
across a stream or logged and piled
in a farmer's field; it lives.
        Willow drives roots down
from bleached and crumbling flesh,
sends slender shoots up to jostle
for sun, to grow lusty leaves
that tremble with the force they hold.
        Alive, it insists when the wind blows,
                                alive.

I could burrow
        into willow's charcoaled heart,
draw deep of its smoky breath,
bend to follow the split where it arches
over the stream to bury its head
in the muddy bank.
        I could settle into its deep creases,
slow my breath in time to its growing,
could learn the rhythms of crumbling
into earth and feel the force of new shoots
driving upwards to insist
                        alive!

CARD SHARP

Cunning, we never caught her cheating
at cards. No aces up her sleeves nor tucked
in the leg of her bloomers; no mirrors
at sneaky angles nor thumb-nailed corners.

Rummy in the evenings and cribbage
with the old man, used matchsticks
marching along holes on the worn board.
On Boxing Day, always Newmarket,
old pennies and ha'pennies saved
for betting on the picture cards
from another pack laid out
in the centre of the drop-leaf table.

Calls of *Nanny! You're cheating!*
made her grin or cackle
as the pennies piled up at her elbow
and her glass of stout emptied,
creamy froth making patterns
like tea-leaves for reading.

Remonstrations of *Really, Mother!*
brought winks and gurning,
her sideways twinkle at us
making sure we knew she cheated
when it didn't matter.

WINDFALLS

I fill a bucket with windfalls and tip them
into the compost. I'll climb a ladder
for the ones on the tree; leave a boxful
by the gate with a sign to *Help Yourself.*
I'll wrap the best in newspaper,
gentled into a carton in the shed.

Autumn brought apples. Green bramleys
for cooking, stewed with blackberries
we gathered in a stain of pricked fingers
and nettle-stung shins. Our favourites
always the sweet Cox's, red-streaked
and crisp. All picked from the ground,
the good ones on the tree kept for market.

Small holes made by beaks or wasps
could be cut out easily; a shallow slice
or a knife-point circled through the skin
to remove a perfect cone. Without a knife,
they could be eaten around, nibbled close
to the edge. The damage didn't go far.

Tiny grub holes hid a deeper harm;
their tracks winding through the flesh,
evading the slicing blade or digging point.
You could cut away half the fruit, chasing the trail.
It wasn't the little tunnels that worried me
but what lay at the heart of each one.

How to Make Paper Flowers

Sit in a garden, wait
until nothing is happening.
Practise amnesia for Latin names.
Bury the memories of your grandmother
pointing out windflowers, love-in-a-mist,
palsywort, gillyflowers and ox-eye.

Don't think of your grandfather's
chrysantheums, cradled in newspaper
and tied to his bike's handlebars
as he rattles home from the allotment,
or of the daisy-chain you hung
round your father's neck.

Only study shape, measure leaf length
against your palm, petals by your fingers.
Don't name colours or compare them
to anything live, forget sonnets on roses
and nursery rhymes.

Choose paper by its texture,
pick cool shades,
light against your cheek.
Smooth it on your lap.
Let your fingers show you
what they've learned.

PLACEMENT

Immersed in writings of diaspora, of displacement,
I sip at not-belonging, roll it around my tongue,
swallow it down and let it lie heavy in my stomach.
The taste is familiar and strange, comfort food
with exotic spices and the sting of hot peppers;
indigestible, irresistible.

                    I could wear a shirt of nettles,
a skirt of thorn; I could stumble with my shoes
on the wrong feet or dress in winter wool
in a heat wave. I could practice braiding my words
with accents, learn to forget names, traditions,
places of family.
              My step reads the path as it spells out
You only have one country.

BLINK

My dad sits cross-legged on the floor in the circle
of small girls passing-the-parcel. He plays the fool,
making my guests giggle and shriek, winks at me
and I can't find the words to say how good this is
but I'm lit up like the candles on my birthday cake.
I close my eyes to make a wish,

open them at the school gate; my skirt is shortened
by rolls at the waist, my stance consciously casual.
My dad's not as wonderful now as the man I wait for
and I hope he'll come while other girls are still there
to see me put on the tossed helmet and take my place
on the pillion. Out of town, the wind hurts my face;
I tuck my head down, shelter behind his leathered back,

look up from my seat on the doorstep. I watch my child
playing in the long grass, think about my dad as granddad,
if he'd lived longer. I twist my wedding ring, not ready
to take it off; try not to think about the fuel bill,
the fences that need mending and the bank's pressing calls.
I know we'll have to leave this place soon and I lean my head
back against the door jamb, let my eyes close

and open them in a jazz club, the band singing
Happy Birthday. My friends round the table warm me,
surprise me, clink glasses and join in with the band.
My child is an adult, my house all mine, and I want
to go home where a poem waits in a notebook
and mutters in the back of my head. Words clamour
for notice, won't let me close my eyes.

To Whom it May Concern

Please find enclosed a key;
it will unlock a door in every house
I've ever lived in. You can try them all
in turn, ticking them off a list,
or pinball between them,
holding your breath at each one
to hope for the snick
that will let you in.

Please find enclosed a strip
torn from the centre
of a diary page. You can find
my diaries on the bookshelves,
in a box under the bed,
and crated at the self-storage
depot. You can look for half-words
to match, the same shade of ink.
A lot of the pages are torn
and crumpled; I don't remember
how, or when.

HIDE AND SEEK

As a child, I hated the foolish feeling
of being found; the too-narrow tree,
the cupboard door that wouldn't close
from inside though my fingertips gripped
to whiteness on a slim batten, the shudder
in my chest when I suppressed noisy breath.

I worked at being lost, taught my joints to fold
and squeeze in small spaces, schooled my breath
to ease, my heart to slow. It took years to train
my blood-flow to thin or pool under my skin,
to shade and pattern the surface.

I hide as a party trick, challenge strangers
in bars to find me; vanish at work, disappear
on dates. I was filmed for a documentary,
shut in an empty room, slowly fading into wallpaper.
I hide from taxes and utility bills, civil suits
and parking tickets.

My house is riddled with small spaces
under floorboards, hollows in cavity walls,
false walls in alcoves. I've perfected the art
of cupboard backs; *trompe l'oeil* on high shelves
with dusty suitcases, sports equipment
and a carefully woven cobweb of nylon fibre.

The fit is perfect, handles on the back
to pull it tight, a can of silicon sealant
stops even my scent from betraying me.
I make my muscles relax, my limbs
settle into their contortions. I wait
for someone who'll seek.

A Telling

Tell me Nanny, why the hares dance in the field
They're waking the seeds in the ground girl,
                calling on the Spring
Tell me Nanny, why you watch the fireback
It draws the things that are gone girl,
                and some things yet to come
Tell me Nanny, why new shoes can't sit on the table
They'll bring a hanging on us girl,
                or the path that leads to one
Tell me Nanny, why we can't have anything green
It calls to the old gentry girl,
                and we don't need noticing by them
Tell me Nanny, why you cover your head under the moon
It would moon-calf and addle-pate me girl,
                take me where I can't come back.
Tell me Nanny, why you don't like to hear the wind blow
Don't you hear it call my name, girl,
                don't you hear it howl my name?

ACKNOWLEDGEMENTS

Poems have been published in the following journals: *Angle, Ink Sweat & Tears, Hearing Voices, Agenda, Brittle Star, Poetry Review* and *Orbis,* and have also appeared in the anthology *Poetic Pilgrimages* (Poetry Salzburg, 2011).

'Prospect' and a version of 'Hide and Seek' were first published in the pamphlet *Lessons in Mallemaroking* (Nine Arches Press, 2011).

'The Visit' was the winner of the Lightship Poetry Prize, 2011.